GARLIC
Cookbook

Printed in the USA by G&R Publishing Co., Waverly, IA

Published and distributed by:

Products

507 Industrial Street
Waverly, IA 50677

ISBN-13: 978-1-56383-271-0
ISBN-10: 1-56383-271-2
Item #3722

Garlic is a vegetable that is a species of the onion family Alliaceae. It is closely related to the onion, shallot and leek. Garlic has a characteristic flavor, making it a popular ingredient for cooking and seasoning. One head of garlic contains several individual cloves of garlic. The leaves and stems (scapes) of the garlic are sometimes eaten, particularly while they are tender and prior to flowering.

Head of Garlic

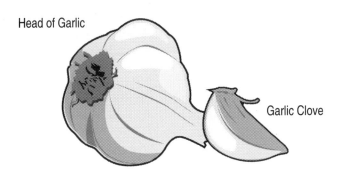

Garlic Clove

Appetizers & Sauces

Roasted Garlic

10 medium heads garlic   3 T. olive oil

Preheat oven to 400°. Arrange the heads of garlic on a baking sheet or place 1 inside each cup of a muffin tin. Drizzle olive oil over heads of garlic. Bake for 40 minutes to 1 hour. The garlic is done when it is soft and squeezable. Remove from oven and let cool slightly before serving. To serve, separate into individual cloves, squeeze the garlic from each clove and spread over toast or crackers. Makes about 15 servings.

Pickled Garlic

½ lb. garlic, peeled
1 large red bell pepper, chopped
2 C. white vinegar

⅔ C. sugar
½ tsp. dry mustard powder
½ tsp. celery seed

In a medium bowl, place peeled garlic cloves. Cut any large cloves in half. Mix in the chopped red bell pepper. In a large saucepan over medium-high heat, place the white vinegar and sugar. Wrap dry mustard and celery seed in a cheesecloth bag and place in the liquid mixture. Bring to a boil. Boil for 5 minutes. Stir in the garlic cloves and red bell pepper. Continue to boil for an additional 5 minutes. Remove from heat and discard cheesecloth bag. Using a slotted spoon, place garlic and red bell peppers in containers to within 1″ of the top. Pour liquid over garlic in containers to within ¼″ from the top. Seal tightly and store in refrigerator for up to 3 weeks.

Garlic Olive Tapenade

1 (6 oz.) can sliced black olives, drained   ¼ tsp. pepper
1 clove garlic, minced   1 T. olive oil
½ tsp. dried basil   3 T. grated Parmesan cheese

In a small bowl, combine drained olives, minced garlic, dried basil and pepper. Stir in olive oil and Parmesan cheese. Mix until well combined, cover and refrigerate for at least 1 hour before serving. To serve, spread tapenade over toasted garlic bread or crackers. Makes 6 to 8 servings.

Stuffed Hot Pepper Snacks

⅓ C. ground Italian sausage
1 (8 oz.) pkg. cream cheese, softened
¾ T. garlic salt
3 T. grated Romano cheese
1 tsp. dried oregano

1 tsp. dried basil
⅓ C. Italian-style dry bread crumbs
1 T. olive oil
6 hot peppers, cored and seeded

Preheat oven to 350°. In a large skillet over medium-high heat, cook sausage until evenly browned. Drain grease from skillet. Crumble sausage. In a medium bowl, combine crumbled sausage, cream cheese, garlic salt, Romano cheese, oregano, basil, bread crumbs and olive oil; mix well. Stuff the peppers with the sausage mixture. Place stuffed peppers on a baking sheet and bake for 20 to 25 minutes, or until the stuffing is lightly browned. Makes 6 servings.

Crab Stuffed Mushrooms

12 large mushrooms, stems removed
1 (6 oz.) pkg. chicken-flavored dry
   stuffing mix
2 C. butter
2 cloves garlic, peeled and minced

1 (8 oz.) pkg. cream cheese, softened
½ lb. real or imitation crabmeat, flaked
Salt and pepper to taste
Crushed red pepper flakes to taste

Preheat oven to 350°. On a baking sheet, arrange mushroom caps bottom side up. Chop and reserve the mushroom stems. Prepare dry stuffing mix according to package directions. In a medium saucepan over medium heat, melt butter. Stir in minced garlic and sauté until tender. In a medium bowl, mix together chopped mushroom stems, prepared stuffing, cream cheese and crabmeat. Stuff mushroom caps generously with the mixture. Drizzle butter and garlic over stuffing and season with salt, pepper, garlic powder and crushed red pepper. Bake for 10 to 12 minutes or until stuffing is lightly browned. Makes 12 servings.

Garlic Butter

¼ C. butter
2 medium cloves garlic, crushed

2 tsp. finely minced parsley
1 tsp. lemon juice

In a small bowl, gently combine butter, crushed garlic, minced parsley and lemon juice. If desired, add more crushed garlic to taste. Pour off any extra lemon juice. Refrigerate until firm.

Garlic Pastry Bites

½ C. self-rising flour
½ tsp. dry mustard powder
2 cloves garlic, crushed
¼ C. butter

¼ C. shredded sharp Cheddar cheese
1 T. cold water
Salt to taste

Into a medium bowl, sift flour. Mix in the dry mustard powder and crushed garlic. Using a pastry blender or two knives, cut in the butter. Add cheese, a little at a time, while slowly blending the butter into the flour. Continue to mix, adding a little cold water if necessary to make a lump of pastry dough. Refrigerate pastry for 15 minutes. Preheat oven to 400°. Roll out pastry on a lightly floured flat surface to form an 8″ square. Cut the pastry into eighths in both directions to form 64 small squares. Transfer the squares to a lightly greased baking sheet, leaving a little room between each square. Sprinkle a little salt over top. Bake for 10 to 15 minutes. Remove from oven and let cool before serving. Makes 64 bites.

Garlic Croutons

2 cloves garlic, minced   3 slices bread, cut into ½˝ cubes
¼ C. butter, melted

Preheat oven to 300°. In a large bowl, combine minced garlic and melted butter. Add the cubes of bread and toss gently until evenly coated. Arrange bread cubes in an even layer on an ungreased baking sheet. Bake for 15 minutes, turning croutons over half way through baking time. Remove from oven and let cool before serving.

Easy Garlic Pretzels

1 C. butter
2 T. Worcestershire sauce
2 T. garlic powder

1 (1 oz.) env. dry onion soup mix
Dash of hot pepper sauce
1 (20 oz.) pkg. sourdough pretzels

Preheat oven to 250°. In a medium saucepan over medium heat, melt butter. Stir in Worcestershire sauce, garlic powder, onion soup mix and hot pepper sauce. Add pretzels to saucepan in batches and toss until evenly coated. Place coated pretzels in an even layer on a baking sheet. Bake for 1 hour, stirring after every 15 minutes. Remove from oven and cool before storing in an airtight container. Makes 12 to 15 servings.

Creamy Garlic Sauce

½ C. water, divided
2 T. minced garlic
1 tsp. garlic powder
2 C. heavy cream

1 T. chopped fresh parsley
Salt and pepper to taste
2 T. cornstarch

In a medium saucepan over medium heat, place ¼ cup water. Bring to a boil. Add minced garlic and garlic powder. Continue to boil until almost all of the water has evaporated, about 5 minutes. Stir in the heavy cream, chopped parsley, salt and pepper. In a small bowl, combine the cornstarch and remaining ¼ cup water; stir into the saucepan. Cook, stirring constantly, until sauce is thick, about 3 minutes. Serve over pasta, chicken or steaks. Makes about 4 servings.

Garlic Hummus

2 cloves garlic, divided
1 (19 oz.) can garbanzo beans in liquid
4 T. lemon juice
2 T. tahini*

1 tsp. salt
Pepper to taste
2 T. olive oil

In a blender or food processor, chop 1 garlic clove. Drain half of the liquid from the garbanzo beans. Pour the remaining liquid and beans into the blender. Add lemon juice, tahini, remaining garlic clove and salt in blender. Cover and blend until creamy. Transfer the mixture to a medium serving bowl. Sprinkle with pepper and drizzle with olive oil. To serve, spread hummus over pita crisps or crackers. Makes 12 to 15 servings.

*Tahini, or sesame paste, is a common ingredient of hummus and other Middle Eastern and East Asian foods. It is sold fresh or dehydrated. Peanut butter can be used as a substitute for tahini, or the ingredient can be omitted.

Spicy Cheese Dip

1 lb. shredded mozzarella cheese
1 C. mayonnaise
3 cloves garlic, minced
1 (2.25 oz.) can sliced black olives, drained

2 fresh jalapeno peppers, seeded and diced, divided
1 tsp. garlic salt

Preheat oven to 350°. In a medium bowl, combine shredded cheese, mayonnaise, minced garlic, drained black olives and 1 of the diced jalapenos. Mix well and spread mixture into an 8″ square baking dish. Season with garlic salt. Sprinkle remaining diced jalapeno over top. Bake for 20 minutes or until edges are golden brown. Makes 12 servings.

Baked Bleu Cheese Dip

½ lb. bacon, chopped
1 tsp. minced garlic
3 (8 oz.) pkgs. cream cheese, softened

4 oz. bleu cheese
¼ C. chopped walnuts or pecans

Preheat oven to 350°. In a large skillet over medium-high heat, sauté chopped bacon until almost done. Stir in minced garlic and sauté for 1 minute. Drain grease from skillet and transfer bacon and minced garlic to a medium bowl. Add cream cheese and bleu cheese. Mix well and transfer to a medium baking dish. Sprinkle chopped nuts over top. Bake for 30 to 40 minutes. Serve with chips, crackers or veggies for dipping. Makes 12 servings.

Quick Guacamole

1 medium ripe avocado,
   peeled and cubed
1 T. salsa

1 clove garlic, peeled
¼ tsp. salt

In a blender or food processor, combine cubed avocado, salsa, garlic clove and salt. Cover and process until smooth. Transfer to a bowl and refrigerate until ready to serve. Stir well before serving. Makes 4 to 6 servings.

Veggie Tomato Sauce

¼ C. olive oil

1 large onion, peeled and coarsely chopped

1 large carrot, peeled and coarsely chopped

3 cloves garlic, peeled and minced

5 large tomatoes, coarsely chopped or 2 (28 oz.) cans whole tomatoes, drained and coarsely chopped

2 T. tomato paste

Coarse salt and pepper to taste

In a large, deep skillet over medium-high heat, heat olive oil. Add chopped onion and carrot and sauté for 2 to 3 minutes. Reduce heat to medium, cover and heat vegetables for about 25 minutes or until soft and golden. Stir in the minced garlic, cover and heat for 5 minutes or until garlic is softened. Add the chopped tomatoes and tomato paste. Bring to a boil, reduce heat and simmer over medium-low heat for about 10 minutes. If a smooth sauce is preferred, strain sauce through a small-holed sieve or puree in a blender or food processor. Add salt and pepper to taste. Sauce can be cooled and stored in the refrigerator for up to 1 week or frozen for up to 3 months. Makes 6 to 8 servings.

Cheesy Garlic Fondue

1 lb. shredded Swiss cheese
½ lb. grated Gruyere cheese
3 T. flour
1 tsp. ground nutmeg
½ tsp. ground white pepper

1¼ C. dry white wine, divided
3 large cloves garlic, minced
1 (1 lb.) loaf crusty French bread,
    cut into 1″ cubes

In a large bowl, combine shredded Swiss cheese, grated Gruyere cheese, flour, nutmeg and white pepper. Toss together until well coated. In a large saucepan over low heat, place 1 cup of white wine and the minced garlic; bring to a simmer. Add cheese mixture by handfuls, whisking until cheese is melted and smooth before adding more. Mix in additional wine by tablespoonfuls until desired consistency is achieved. Transfer cheese mixture to a fondue pot; set over candle or canned heat. Serve with bread cubes for dipping. Makes 8 to 10 servings.

Twice Tomato Bruschetta

6 plum tomatoes, chopped
½ C. chopped oil-packed sun-dried
   tomatoes
3 cloves garlic, minced
¼ C. olive oil
2 T. balsamic vinegar

¼ C. chopped fresh basil,
   stems removed
¼ tsp. salt
¼ tsp. pepper
1 French baguette
2 C. shredded mozzarella cheese

Preheat oven broiler. In a large bowl, combine chopped plum tomatoes, sun-dried tomatoes, minced garlic, olive oil, balsamic vinegar, chopped basil, salt and pepper. Mix lightly and let sit for 10 minutes. Cut the French baguette into ¾″ thick slices. Place the slices in a single layer on a baking sheet. Place baking sheet about 6″ under broiler for 1 to 2 minutes, or until slightly browned. Divide tomato mixture evenly over baguette slices and top with mozzarella cheese. Return to broiler for 2 to 3 minutes or until cheese is melted. Makes 10 to 12 servings.

Baked Spinach Cups

2 (10 oz.) pkgs. frozen chopped
   spinach, thawed
1 egg, beaten
2 cloves garlic, finely minced

1 (8 oz.) pkg. crumbled feta cheese
3 (2 oz.) pkgs. pre-baked mini phyllo
   dough shells

Preheat oven to 400°. Wrap the thawed spinach in paper towels and squeeze over the sink to remove any liquid. In a large bowl, combine the egg, minced garlic and feta cheese. Stir in the spinach; mix until well combined. Place the phyllo shells in a single layer on a baking sheet. Divide the spinach mixture evenly into the phyllo shells. Bake for 6 to 8 minutes or until heated through. Makes 9 servings.

Breads

The Best Garlic Bread

½ C. butter, softened
2 T. mayonnaise
¼ tsp. dried sage
3 cloves garlic, minced
2 tsp. dried oregano

½ tsp. salt
½ tsp. pepper
1 (1 lb.) loaf French bread,
   halved lengthwise
2 T. grated Parmesan cheese

Preheat oven broiler. In a medium bowl, combine butter, mayonnaise, sage, minced garlic, oregano, salt and pepper; mix well. Spread mixture evenly over bread halves. Sprinkle grated Parmesan cheese over top. Place bread directly on oven rack about 6″ under broiler for 5 minutes, or until the bread is lightly toasted. Cut each bread half into 2″ or 3″ slices. Makes 6 to 8 servings.

Cheesy Onion Garlic Bread

2 French baguettes
¼ C. butter
1 large onion, minced
8 cloves garlic, minced

2 C. shredded mozzarella cheese
½ C. grated Parmesan cheese
1 C. mayonnaise

Preheat oven broiler. Slice the French baguettes into ¾″ thick slices. In a medium skillet over medium heat, melt the butter. Add the minced onion and minced garlic; sauté until tender. Remove from heat and let cool to room temperature. In a medium bowl, combine mozzarella cheese, Parmesan cheese and mayonnaise. Arrange the bread slices in a single layer on a baking sheet. Spread onion and garlic mixture evenly over bread slices and place baking sheet about 6″ under broiler for 5 minutes or until cheese is melted and lightly browned. Serve immediately. Makes 8 to 10 servings.

Herbed Parmesan Garlic Bread

½ C. butter, melted
1 tsp. garlic salt
¼ tsp. dried rosemary
⅛ tsp. dried basil
⅛ tsp. dried thyme

⅛ tsp. garlic powder
1 T. grated Parmesan cheese
1 (1 lb.) loaf French bread,
  halved lengthwise

Preheat oven to 300°. In a small bowl, combine melted butter, garlic salt, rosemary, basil, thyme, garlic powder and Parmesan cheese. Use a pastry brush to spread mixture evenly over French bread halves. If desired, sprinkle with additional Parmesan cheese. Place bread halves on a baking sheet. Bake for 10 to 12 minutes or until the edges of the bread are lightly browned. Cut each bread half into 2″ or 3″ slices. Makes 6 servings.

Veggie Lover's Garlic Bread

1 clove garlic, minced
⅛ C. olive oil
1 medium eggplant, cubed
1 zucchini, cubed
1 medium tomato, peeled and chopped
1 tsp. salt

2 tsp. minced fresh oregano
2 tsp. minced fresh basil
1 French baguette
4 tsp. garlic powder
6 tsp. butter, softened

In a large skillet over medium heat, sauté minced garlic in olive oil until golden brown, about 2 minutes. Add cubed eggplant and cubed zucchini and sauté until tender, about 5 to 7 minutes. Add the chopped tomato and continue to heat, stirring often, until the tomato becomes a pulp. Mix in the salt, oregano and basil and heat for an additional 2 minutes. Remove from heat and cool to room temperature. Preheat oven to 325°. Slice the French baguette into 1″ slices. Sprinkle garlic powder over each slice. Place the bread slices directly on the oven rack at heat for 3 to 5 minutes. Remove toasted slices and arrange on a serving platter. Top slices evenly with vegetable mixture. Makes 6 to 8 servings.

Bleu Cheese Ponderosas

1 C. butter
5½ T. minced garlic
2½ T. crumbled bleu cheese
3½ T. herbes de Provence

1 T. crushed red pepper flakes
Coarse salt and pepper to taste
Dash of Worcestershire sauce
1 French baguette

Preheat outdoor grill to high heat. In a medium saucepan over medium heat, melt the butter. Mix in the minced garlic, bleu cheese, herbes de Provence, red pepper flakes, salt, pepper and Worcestershire sauce. Cut the baguette into thick slices. Dunk each baguette slice in the melted butter mixture, turning to coat all sides. Place the coated baguette slices on the prepared grill. Grill for 1 to 2 minutes on each side or to desired doneness. Makes 10 to 12 servings.

Bubble Garlic Loaf

¼ C. butter, melted
1 T. dried parsley
1 tsp. garlic powder

¼ tsp. garlic salt
1 (1 lb.) loaf frozen white bread
dough, thawed

Grease a 5 x 9″ loaf pan. In a medium bowl, combine melted butter, parsley, garlic powder and garlic salt; mix well. Cut the bread dough into 1″ pieces. Dip the dough pieces into the butter mixture and layer them into the greased loaf pan. Cover pan and let dough rise until doubled in size, about 1 hour. Preheat oven to 350°. Bake for 30 minutes or until golden brown. To serve, remove bubble loaf from pan and pull pieces of bread from the loaf. Makes 10 to 12 servings.

Parmesan Bread Ring

1 (1 lb.) loaf frozen white bread dough, thawed
¾ C. butter, melted
1 egg, beaten

¼ C. grated Parmesan cheese
1 tsp. garlic powder
1 tsp. salt
1 tsp. dried parsley

Lightly grease a 9˝ Bundt cake pan. Pull 1˝ pieces from the bread dough loaf and roll into balls. In a medium bowl, combine melted butter and egg. Mix in Parmesan cheese, garlic powder, salt and dried parsley. Dip dough balls into butter mixture and layer into the greased Bundt pan. Cover pan and let dough rise until doubled in size, about 1 hour. Preheat oven to 350°. Bake until golden brown, about 35 minutes. Makes 10 to 12 servings.

Garlic Breadstick Twists

1 (10 oz.) tube refrigerated pizza
   crust dough
⅓ C. olive oil
6 T. minced garlic

5 T. grated Parmesan cheese
3 T. chopped fresh parsley
1 tsp. crushed red pepper flakes
1 tsp. salt

Preheat oven to 450°. Grease a baking sheet or line with parchment paper. Roll out pizza dough into a 9 x 16″ rectangle. Use a pizza wheel to cut the dough into ¾″ thick strips of dough along the 9″ side. Cut each strip in half, forming 24 pieces. Twist each strip of dough or tie into a knot. Place dough twists on baking sheet. Bake for 10 to 12 minutes or until golden brown. Remove twists from oven and place in a large bowl. Drizzle olive oil over twists and sprinkle with minced garlic, Parmesan cheese, parsley, red pepper flakes and salt. Toss until evenly coated and serve. Makes 24 twists.

Garlic Cheddar Biscuits

2 C. biscuit baking mix
1 C. shredded Cheddar cheese
½ tsp. garlic powder
⅔ C. milk

2 T. butter, melted
2 tsp. dried parsley
1 tsp. garlic salt

Preheat oven to 400°. Grease a baking sheet or line with parchment paper. In a large bowl, combine baking mix, Cheddar cheese and garlic powder. Stir in milk until a dough forms. Drop dough by heaping tablespoonfuls onto baking sheet. Bake for 10 minutes. Remove from oven and use a pastry brush to cover biscuits with melted butter. Sprinkle with dried parsley and garlic salt. Return to oven for 5 minutes or until biscuits are lightly browned on the bottom. Makes 8 to 10 biscuits.

Fried Pita Crisps

2 T. butter, divided
1 T. olive oil
2 T. lemon juice, divided

2 T. minced garlic
½ T. garlic powder
2 (4″) pita bread rounds

In a medium skillet over low heat, melt 1 tablespoon butter. Mix in the olive oil, 1 tablespoon lemon juice, minced garlic and garlic powder. Cut each pita in half and then along the edge to divide into single layers. Next, cut each pita half into 4 triangles. Place the pita triangles in the skillet and top with remaining butter and lemon juice. Heat for about 10 minutes, turning often, until golden brown. Serve immediately. Makes 10 to 16 servings.

Side Dishes

Garlic Corn on the Cob

12 ears corn, husked and cleaned   ¼ C. garlic powder
¾ C. butter, divided

Preheat oven to 350° or outdoor grill to medium heat. Cut 12 squares of aluminum foil. Place each cleaned ear of corn on a piece of aluminum foil. Place 1 tablespoon of butter over each one and sprinkle with garlic powder. Wrap ears tightly with aluminum foil. Place ears of corn on the grill or directly on oven rack for 20 to 30 minutes, turning over occasionally. Makes 12 servings.

Spicy Green Beans

¾ lb. fresh green beans, trimmed
2 T. soy sauce
1 clove garlic, minced

1 tsp. garlic chili sauce
1 tsp. honey
2 tsp. vegetable oil

In a steamer basket over a pot of boiling water, steam the green beans for 3 to 4 minutes. In a medium bowl, combine the soy sauce, minced garlic, chili sauce and honey. In a medium skillet over medium heat, place the vegetable oil. Add the steamed green beans and fry for 3 to 5 minutes. Add the soy sauce mixture and continue to heat for 2 minutes, stirring often, until almost all of the liquid has evaporated. Makes 4 servings.

Garlic Broccoli Salad

4 cloves garlic, peeled
1½ tsp. salt
⅓ C. olive oil
¼ C. red wine vinegar

1 T. Dijon mustard
1 large bunch broccoli, cut into florets
½ C. grated Parmesan cheese

In a mortar dish or small bowl, place the garlic cloves. Sprinkle with salt. Mash with a pestle or the back of a spoon to form a paste. Transfer garlic paste to a medium bowl and stir in olive oil, red wine vinegar and Dijon mustard. Add the broccoli florets and toss until evenly coated. Chill for at least 3 hours, tossing occasionally. Sprinkle with Parmesan cheese just before serving. Makes 8 servings.

Baked Garlic Broccoli

1 large bunch broccoli
1 small onion, chopped
8 cloves garlic, minced
½ C. olive oil

1 C. dry bread crumbs
¾ C. grated Parmesan cheese
1 egg, lightly beaten
Salt and pepper to taste

Preheat oven to 350°. In a steamer basket over a pot of boiling water, steam the broccoli until tender or boil broccoli in a pot of water. Drain broccoli and return to pot. Mash broccoli with a potato masher. In a medium saucepan over medium heat, sauté chopped onion and minced garlic in olive oil. Once onions are translucent, add mashed broccoli to pot and mix until well combined. Add bread crumbs and Parmesan cheese and mix until blended. Remove from heat and stir in egg. Season with salt and pepper to taste. Transfer mixture to a greased 8″ square baking dish. Bake for 15 to 20 minutes. Makes 6 servings.

Broccoli & Noodles

6 C. uncooked wide noodles
3 cloves garlic, minced
¼ C. olive oil
4 C. broccoli florets

½ lb. fresh mushrooms, thinly sliced
½ tsp. dried thyme
¼ tsp. pepper
1 tsp. salt

In a large pot of lightly salted water over medium-high heat, bring water to a boil. Add noodles and cook for 8 to 10 minutes or until pasta is soft but firm. Drain water from pot and set aside. In a large skillet over medium-high heat, sauté minced garlic in olive oil until tender. Add broccoli florets and continue to sauté for 4 minutes or until tender but crisp. Add the sliced mushrooms, thyme, pepper and salt and continue to sauté for 2 to 3 minutes. Add noodles to broccoli mixture and toss until well combined and heated through. Makes 6 to 8 servings.

Steamed Garlic Zucchini

4 zucchini   1 T. olive oil
2 cloves garlic

Bring a large pot of water to a boil. Trim ends from zucchini and cut each in half. Cut each half into quarters. In a steamer basket over a pot of boiling water, steam the zucchini pieces for 10 to 15 minutes or until tender. Transfer zucchini to a large bowl. Mash the garlic into a paste using a mortar and pestle or the back of a spoon. Add to the bowl with zucchini. Drizzle with olive oil and toss until zucchini is evenly coated. Makes 4 servings.

Cheddar Zucchini Casserole

4 slices bread, cubed
¼ C. butter, melted
2 C. cubed zucchini
1 large onion, chopped

1 tsp. garlic salt
1 egg, beaten
2 C. shredded Cheddar cheese

Preheat oven to 350°. In a medium bowl, place bread cubes. Pour melted butter over top. Add cubed zucchini, chopped onion, garlic salt and egg. Mix until well combined. Transfer mixture to a lightly greased 9 x 13″ baking dish. Sprinkle Cheddar cheese over top. Bake for 30 minutes. Cover dish with aluminum foil and bake for an additional 30 minutes. Makes 4 to 6 servings.

Sautéed Herbed Mushrooms

1 T. olive oil
1½ lbs. fresh button mushrooms
1 tsp. Italian seasoning
¼ C. dry white wine

2 cloves garlic, minced
Salt and pepper to taste
2 T. chopped fresh chives

In a large skillet over medium heat, place olive oil. Add fresh mushrooms to skillet and sprinkle with Italian seasoning. Sauté for 10 minutes, stirring often. Mix in the white wine and minced garlic; continue to heat until most of the wine has evaporated. Season with salt and pepper and sprinkle chopped chives over top. Continue to heat for 1 minute. Serve immediately. Makes 4 to 6 servings.

Garlic Lime Asparagus

1 tsp. butter
1 T. olive oil
1 clove garlic, minced
1 medium shallot, minced

1 bunch fresh asparagus spears,
  trimmed
1 lime, quartered
Salt and pepper to taste

In a large skillet over medium heat, place butter and olive oil. Once butter is melted, stir in minced garlic and minced shallot; sauté for 1 to 2 minutes. Stir in asparagus spears and cook until tender, about 5 minutes. Squeeze 1 of the lime quarters over asparagus in skillet and season with salt and pepper to taste. Transfer sautéed asparagus to a serving platter and garnish with remaining lime wedges. Serve immediately. Makes 4 servings.

Vegetable Medley with Almonds

½ C. butter
1 tsp. garlic salt
1 tsp. garlic pepper*
2 T. sliced almonds
2 T. dry white wine

1 medium onion, chopped
1 medium red bell pepper, chopped
2 C. chopped broccoli
2 C. chopped cauliflower

In a large skillet over medium-low heat, place butter. Once butter is melted, add garlic salt and garlic pepper. Mix in sliced almonds and heat until almonds are golden brown. Stir in white wine, chopped onion, chopped red pepper, chopped broccoli and chopped cauliflower. Sauté for 5 minutes, stirring often, until vegetables are tender and heated through. Serve immediately. Makes 4 to 6 servings.

*Garlic pepper is a common meat or vegetable seasoning. It is a combination of garlic, salt, pepper, brown sugar, dried onion, dried bell pepper and dried parsley.

The Ultimate Garlic Mashed Potatoes

3 lbs. Yukon Gold or russet potatoes
½ C. heavy cream
½ C. whole milk
2 T. butter

2 cloves garlic
¼ tsp. ground nutmeg
¼ tsp. ground white pepper
Salt to taste

Peel and quarter the potatoes. In a large pot of boiling water over medium-high heat, cook potatoes until tender. Remove from heat, drain water and return potatoes to pot. Add heavy cream, whole milk and butter. Mash potatoes with a potato masher until desired consistency is achieved. Use a garlic press to squeeze the garlic cloves into the mashed potatoes. Add nutmeg, white pepper and salt to taste. Blend until thoroughly combined. If a creamier consistency is desired, stir in more cream or milk. If a milder garlic taste is desired, boil the garlic cloves with the potatoes. Makes 6 servings.

Red Garlic Mashed Potatoes

8 medium red potatoes, quartered
2 tsp. crushed garlic, divided
½ C. butter
¼ C. half-and-half

2 T. sugar
¼ tsp. steak seasoning
¼ tsp. garlic powder

Do not peel the potatoes. Place the quartered potatoes in a large pot and fill with enough water to cover the potatoes. Place over medium-high heat and bring the potatoes to a boil. Add 1 teaspoon of crushed garlic to the water and cook for about 10 minutes, or until the potatoes pierce easily with a fork. Remove from heat, drain water and return potatoes to pot. Add the butter. Mash potatoes with a potato masher and add half-and-half, sugar, steak seasoning, garlic powder and remaining 1 teaspoon crushed garlic. Continue to mash potatoes or mix with an electric mixer until desired consistency is achieved. Makes 4 servings.

Garlic Scalloped Potatoes

1 (10.75 oz.) can Cheddar cheese soup
2 C. half-and-half
2 T. herb and garlic-flavored cream
   cheese, softened
2 T. dried onion flakes
2 T. garlic powder
2 T. dry mustard powder
1 T. chicken bouillon granules

Salt and pepper to taste
6 large baking potatoes, peeled
   and thinly sliced
3 cloves garlic, minced
2 stalks celery, thinly sliced
1½ C. shredded Cheddar cheese
½ C. grated Parmesan cheese

Preheat oven to 350°. In a large bowl, combine cheese soup, half-and-half, cream cheese, onion flakes, garlic powder, mustard powder, chicken bouillon, salt and pepper. Grease a 9 x 13˝ baking dish. Layer ⅓ of the potato slices across the bottom of the dish, overlapping slightly. Sprinkle half of the minced garlic and half of the sliced celery over the potatoes. Repeat layers and top with final ⅓ of the potato slices. Pour cheese soup mixture over potatoes, spreading evenly. Cover tightly with aluminum foil. Bake for 45 minutes. Uncover and sprinkle Cheddar and Parmesan cheese over top. Return to oven for an additional 20 minutes or until a knife can be easily inserted into potatoes. Makes 8 servings.

Crispy Gold Potatoes

¼ C. olive oil, divided
Salt and pepper to taste
2 lbs. small Yukon Gold potatoes,
    halved

6 medium cloves garlic, thinly sliced
2 T. chopped fresh parsley

Preheat oven to 400°. Brush a baking sheet with 1 tablespoon of the olive oil and sprinkle with salt and pepper. Arrange the halved potatoes over the baking sheet, cut side down. Bake for 45 minutes or until potatoes are crisp and golden brown. Transfer potatoes to a bowl. In a large skillet over medium-low heat, place remaining 3 tablespoons olive oil. Add sliced garlic and heat until just lightly browned. Pour the garlic and oil over the potatoes in the bowl. Add parsley and toss until evenly coated. Season with salt and pepper and serve immediately. Makes 8 servings.

Baked Garlic Hash Browns

8 frozen hash brown patties
1 tsp. salt
½ tsp. garlic powder

1 C. heavy cream
1 C. shredded Cheddar cheese

Preheat oven to 350°. Place hash brown patties in a greased 9 x 13″ baking dish. Sprinkle with salt and garlic powder. Pour cream over patties. Bake for 50 minutes. Sprinkle with Cheddar cheese. Return to oven and bake for an additional 5 to 10 minutes or until potatoes are tender and cheese is melted. Makes 8 servings.

Garlic Rice

2 T. vegetable oil
1½ T. minced garlic
2 T. ground pork

4 C. cooked white rice
1½ tsp. garlic salt
Pepper to taste

In a large skillet over medium-high heat, place the vegetable oil. Once the oil is hot, add the minced garlic and ground pork. Heat, stirring often, until ground pork is cooked and garlic is lightly browned. Stir in the cooked white rice. Season with garlic salt and pepper to taste. Continue to heat until flavors are well blended, about 3 minutes. Makes 4 servings.

Wild Rice & Mushroom Bake

4 C. water
4 beef bouillon cubes
2 cloves garlic, minced
½ C. uncooked wild rice, rinsed

½ C. uncooked long grain rice
1 (4.5 oz.) jar sliced mushrooms, drained
¼ C. butter

In a large saucepan over medium heat, combine water, beef bouillon, minced garlic and wild rice. Bring to a boil, reduce heat, cover and let simmer for 30 minutes. Add long grain rice, cover and simmer for an additional 20 to 25 minutes or until the rice is tender. Preheat oven to 350°. Stir in the sliced mushrooms and butter. Transfer rice mixture to an 8″ square baking dish. Bake for 30 to 40 minutes or until all of the liquid has absorbed. Makes 6 servings.

Garlic Black Beans

1 (16 oz.) can black beans
1 small onion, chopped
1 clove garlic, chopped

1 T. chopped fresh cilantro
¼ tsp. cayenne pepper
Salt to taste

In a medium saucepan over medium heat, combine black beans in liquid, chopped onion and chopped garlic; bring to a boil. Reduce heat to medium-low. Season with cilantro, cayenne pepper and salt. Simmer for 5 minutes. Makes 4 servings.

Spicy Cornbread Stuffing

1 lb. bulk Italian sausage
1 C. chopped celery
1 medium onion, chopped
½ C. chopped carrot
4 to 6 Serrano or jalapeno peppers,
    seeded and chopped

4 cloves garlic, minced
½ tsp. dried thyme
½ tsp. dried sage
6 C. coarsely crumbled cornbread
½ C. chicken broth

Preheat oven to 200°. In a large skillet over medium heat, cook Italian sausage, chopped celery, chopped onion, chopped carrot, chopped peppers and minced garlic. Heat for about 10 minutes or until sausage is cooked and vegetables are tender. Drain grease from skillet and stir in thyme and sage. In a large mixing bowl, combine crumbled cornbread and cooked sausage mixture. Add chicken broth and toss until well moistened. Transfer to a greased 9 x 13″ baking dish and cover with aluminum foil. Bake for 30 minutes. Makes 8 to 10 servings.

Amaretto Spinach Salad

2 lbs. spinach
1 lb. bacon, diced
½ C. vegetable oil
2 large cloves garlic, crushed
½ C. red wine vinegar
½ C. lemon juice

4 tsp. Worcestershire sauce
1 tsp. dry mustard powder
¼ C. amaretto
Salt and pepper to taste
¼ lb. mushrooms, sliced
1 small red onion, sliced

Wash spinach and remove any large stems. Tear spinach into bite-size pieces. In a large skillet over medium heat, cook diced bacon until crisp. Remove bacon from skillet and drain grease, reserving ⅛ cup bacon grease in the skillet. Add vegetable oil, crushed garlic, red wine vinegar, lemon juice, Worcestershire sauce, mustard powder, amaretto, salt and pepper to bacon grease in skillet. Simmer, stirring often, until heated through. In a salad bowl, toss together spinach, sliced mushrooms, sliced red onion and bacon. Right before serving, pour slightly cooled dressing over salad and toss. Serve immediately. Makes 6 to 8 servings.

Creamed Spinach

2 (10 oz.) pkgs. frozen chopped
   spinach, thawed
1 (10.75 oz.) can cream of celery soup
1 T. flour

4 T. butter
½ tsp. garlic salt or minced garlic
Salt and pepper to taste

Wrap the thawed spinach in paper towels and squeeze over the sink to remove any liquid. In a medium saucepan over medium heat, place cream of celery soup. Stir in flour, butter, garlic, salt and pepper. Stir in drained spinach. Cook, stirring often, for 7 to 10 minutes. Serve warm. Makes 4 servings.

Main Dishes

Egg & Sausage Muffins

½ lb. ground pork sausage

12 eggs, beaten

1 (4 oz.) can chopped green chilies, drained

1 small onion, chopped

1 tsp. garlic powder

Salt and pepper to taste

Preheat oven to 350°. Lightly grease 12 muffin cups. In a large, deep skillet over medium-high heat, cook sausage until evenly browned. Remove from heat and drain grease from skillet. In a large bowl, combine beaten eggs, chopped chilies, chopped onion, garlic powder, salt, pepper and browned sausage. Mix until well combined. Spoon ¼ cup of the egg and sausage mixture into each prepared muffin cup. Bake for 15 to 20 minutes or until a toothpick inserted in center of egg cups comes out clean. Serve immediately. Makes 12 servings.

Tomato & Mushroom Brunch Burritos

6 cloves garlic, crushed
1 (8 oz.) pkg. sliced mushrooms
1 tsp. garlic salt
6 eggs, beaten
4 (10˝) flour tortillas

2 C. shredded Monterey Jack cheese, divided
16 cherry tomatoes, halved and divided
1 (5 oz.) pkg. alfalfa sprouts, divided

Generously grease a medium saucepan with butter-flavored cooking spray. Place saucepan over medium heat and sauté garlic for 3 minutes. Stir in the sliced mushrooms and sprinkle with garlic salt. Sauté until mushrooms are tender, about 3 minutes. Transfer garlic and mushrooms to a plate and set aside. In the same saucepan, scramble eggs until half cooked. Return mushrooms and garlic to pan until scrambled eggs are firm. Divide the egg mixture evenly onto the 4 tortillas. Top each tortilla with ½ cup shredded cheese, 8 cherry tomato halves and ¼ of the sprouts. Roll up tortillas and serve. Makes 4 servings.

Artichoke Pie

1 T. olive oil
1 clove garlic, minced
2 (6 oz.) cans artichoke hearts, drained
½ C. Italian seasoned bread crumbs
½ C. grated Parmesan cheese, divided

1 (9˝) unbaked pie shell
3 eggs, beaten
1 (8 oz.) pkg. shredded mozzarella cheese

Preheat oven to 350°. In a large skillet over medium heat, heat olive oil. Add minced garlic and sauté until just lightly browned. Stir in the artichoke hearts and heat for 10 minutes. Add bread crumbs and ¼ cup Parmesan cheese. Continue to heat for 1 to 2 minutes. Transfer mixture to pie shell. Pour eggs over artichoke mixture and sprinkle with remaining ¼ cup Parmesan cheese. Top with shredded mozzarella cheese. Bake for 45 minutes or until pie crust begins to brown.

Deep-Dish Broccoli Pizza

1 pkg. active dry yeast
1 C. warm water (110° to 115°F)
1 tsp. sugar
3½ C. unbleached flour
1 C. cake flour
1½ tsp. salt
1 C. plus 2 T. olive oil, divided
3 tsp. minced garlic, divided
6 C. peeled, seeded and chopped
   tomatoes
1 tsp. dried oregano

1 tsp. dried basil
2 C. sliced mushrooms
Salt and pepper to taste
2 T. butter
1 lb. Italian sweet sausage
½ tsp. crushed fennel seeds
8 C. chopped broccoli, blanched
1 T. shortening
3½ C. shredded mozzarella cheese,
   divided
½ C. grated Parmesan cheese

Dissolve yeast in warm water and stir in sugar. In a medium bowl, combine unbleached flour, cake flour and salt. Gradually stir in the yeast mixture and ¼ cup olive oil. Knead the dough until smooth and return to the bowl. Cover with plastic wrap and let rise

continued on next page

until tripled in size, about 2 to 3 hours. Meanwhile, in a medium saucepan over medium heat, place ¼ cup olive oil. Add 2 teaspoons minced garlic and sauté for 1 minute. Add tomatoes and heat until thickened, about 45 minutes. Stir in oregano and basil. Transfer sauce to a dish and let cool. Add 2 tablespoons olive oil to same saucepan and sauté mushrooms; season with salt and pepper. Transfer to a dish. Add 2 tablespoons olive oil and butter to same saucepan and cook sausage, fennel seeds and remaining 1 teaspoon minced garlic. Heat for 1 minute and stir in blanched broccoli. When dough has risen, punch down and remove ⅓ of the dough. Preheat oven to 425°. Grease a large deep-dish pizza pan with shortening. Roll out remaining dough to a 20″ circle; fit dough into pan with excess hanging over the side. Brush dough with 1 tablespoon olive oil; sprinkle with salt and 1 cup mozzarella cheese. Spread tomato sauce over cheese and top with mushrooms and 1 cup mozzarella cheese. Roll out remaining dough to a 14″ circle and fit over ingredients in pan, pressing edges together. Trim overhanging dough to ½″, fold inward and crimp to make a raised edge. Cut a few slits in dough for steam to escape and brush with 1 tablespoon olive oil. Spread sausage and broccoli over dough and top with remaining mozzarella and Parmesan cheese. Drizzle with remaining ¼ cup olive oil. Bake for 30 to 40 minutes. Makes 6 to 8 servings.

Garlic Scape Pizza

6 to 8 garlic scapes*, sliced
3 to 4 cloves garlic, minced
½ medium onion, chopped
½ red bell pepper, chopped
½ yellow bell pepper, chopped
2 T. butter
½ (6 oz.) can tomato paste

1 (12″) pre-baked pizza crust
½ C. shredded mozzarella cheese
½ C. fresh spinach
½ C. shredded Cheddar cheese
1 (3 oz.) pkg. sliced pepperoni
10 cherry tomatoes, halved
½ C. shredded Parmesan cheese

Preheat oven to 350°. In a medium saucepan over medium-high heat, sauté garlic scapes, garlic, onion, red pepper and yellow pepper in butter until tender. Spread tomato paste over pizza crust and sprinkle with mozzarella cheese. Spread spinach over cheese and top with sautéed vegetables. Sprinkle Cheddar cheese over top and add sliced pepperoni. Cover with halved tomatoes and sprinkle with Parmesan cheese. Bake for 20 to 25 minutes. Makes 4 to 6 servings.

*Garlic scapes are the flower stalks of a garlic bulb. Garlic scapes curl upward as they grow, straighten and then grow seed-like bulbs. The scapes should be harvested when they are still in full curl and tender.

Garlic Penne Pasta

1 (16 oz.) pkg. uncooked penne pasta
½ C. olive oil
1 medium head garlic, peeled
   and chopped
1 T. chopped fresh basil

1 T. chopped fresh oregano
2 T. chopped fresh parsley
1 T. crushed red pepper flakes
1 C. grated Parmesan cheese

In a large pot of lightly salted water over medium heat, bring water to a boil. Add penne pasta and cook for 8 to 10 minutes or until pasta is al dente. Drain water from pot and transfer cooked pasta to a large bowl. In a medium skillet over low heat, place olive oil. Add chopped garlic and sauté until tender, about 10 to 15 minutes. Stir in basil, oregano, parsley and red pepper flakes. Remove from heat. Pour garlic and herb mixture over pasta and let sit for 3 to 5 minutes. Sprinkle with Parmesan cheese and toss until well combined. Makes 8 servings.

Bacon, Pea & Garlic Spaghetti

1 (16 oz.) pkg. uncooked spaghetti
1 T. olive oil
¼ lb. bacon, diced
1 small onion, chopped
1 clove garlic, minced
2 (15 oz.) cans tomato sauce

1½ tsp. chopped fresh parsley
¼ tsp. dried basil
1 tsp. garlic powder
½ tsp. pepper
1 (15 oz.) can peas, drained
¼ C. grated Romano cheese

In a large pot of lightly salted water over medium heat, bring water to a boil. Add spaghetti and cook for 8 to 10 minutes or until pasta is al dente. Drain water from pot and transfer cooked pasta to a large bowl. In a medium skillet over medium heat, place olive oil. Sauté bacon, onion and garlic in skillet until lightly browned. Stir in tomato sauce, parsley, basil, garlic powder and pepper. Bring to a boil, reduce heat and let simmer for 20 to 30 minutes, stirring occasionally. Mix in drained peas. Pour sauce over spaghetti in bowl and toss. Sprinkle Romano cheese over top. Makes 6 servings.

Light Summer Pasta

1 (16 oz.) pkg. uncooked linguini pasta
6 plum tomatoes, chopped
1 lb. shredded mozzarella cheese
⅓ C. chopped fresh basil

6 cloves garlic, minced
½ C. olive oil
½ tsp. garlic salt
Pepper to taste

In a large pot of lightly salted water over medium heat, bring water to a boil. Add linguini pasta and cook for 8 to 10 minutes or until pasta is al dente. Drain water from pot and transfer cooked pasta to a large bowl. Meanwhile, in a medium bowl, combine chopped tomatoes, mozzarella cheese, basil, minced garlic, olive oil, garlic salt and pepper; mix well. Pour over pasta and toss. Serve immediately. Makes 6 servings.

Tomato & Basil Spaghettini

1 (16 oz.) pkg. uncooked spaghettini
(thin spaghetti)
1 (14.5 oz.) can diced tomatoes
with garlic
2 medium tomatoes, chopped
1 C. fresh basil leaves

4 large cloves garlic
2 T. olive oil
Pepper to taste
1 lemon, juiced
4 oz. soft goat cheese

In a large pot of lightly salted water over medium heat, bring water to a boil. Add spaghettini and cook for 8 to 10 minutes or until pasta is al dente. Drain water from pot and transfer cooked pasta to a large bowl. In a blender or food processor, place diced tomatoes in juice, chopped tomatoes, basil leaves, garlic cloves, olive oil and pepper. Blend until combined but still chunky. Pour over pasta in bowl and toss. Just before serving, sprinkle lemon juice and goat cheese over top. Makes 8 servings.

Easy Chicken Pasta Toss

1 (16 oz.) pkg. uncooked rotini pasta
4 skinless, boneless chicken breast
    halves, cut into 1″ pieces
¼ C. olive oil
3 cloves garlic, minced
1¼ tsp. salt

1¼ tsp. garlic powder
1¼ tsp. dried basil
1¼ tsp. dried oregano
1 C. chopped sun-dried tomatoes
¼ C. grated Parmesan cheese

In a large pot of lightly salted water over medium heat, bring water to a boil. Add rotini pasta and cook for 8 to 10 minutes or until pasta is al dente. Drain water from pot and transfer cooked pasta to a large bowl. Meanwhile, in a large skillet over medium-high heat, sauté chicken pieces in olive oil. Add minced garlic, salt, garlic powder, basil and oregano; continue to sauté until chicken is cooked. Add sun-dried tomatoes and heat for 2 additional minutes. Pour over pasta in bowl and toss. Sprinkle Parmesan cheese over top and serve. Makes 8 servings.

Spinach Tortellini

1 (16 oz.) pkg. uncooked cheese
   tortellini
1 (14.5 oz.) can diced tomatoes
   with garlic
1 C. chopped fresh spinach
½ tsp. salt
¼ tsp. pepper

1½ tsp. dried basil
1 tsp. minced garlic
2 T. flour
¾ C. milk
¾ C. heavy cream
¼ C. grated Parmesan cheese

In a large pot of lightly salted water over medium heat, bring water to a boil. Add tortellini and cook for 8 to 10 minutes or until pasta is al dente. Meanwhile, in a large saucepan over medium heat, combine tomatoes in juice, chopped spinach, salt, pepper, basil and minced garlic. Cook, stirring often, until sauce begins to simmer. In a medium bowl, whisk together flour, milk and heavy cream. Stir cream mixture into tomato mixture and add Parmesan cheese. Continue to cook until thickened and heated through, about 2 minutes. Drain water from tortellini and transfer cooked tortellini to saucepan. Stir until coated and serve. Makes 6 servings.

Garlic Spaghetti Sauce with Meatballs

1 lb. lean ground beef
1 C. fresh bread crumbs
1 T. dried parsley
1 T. grated Parmesan cheese
¾ tsp. pepper, divided
⅛ tsp. garlic powder
1 egg, beaten
¾ C. chopped onion

5 cloves garlic, minced
¼ C. olive oil
2 (28 oz.) cans whole peeled tomatoes
2 tsp. salt
1 tsp. sugar
1 bay leaf
1 (6 oz.) can tomato paste
¾ tsp. dried basil

In a large bowl, combine ground beef, bread crumbs, parsley, Parmesan cheese, ¼ teaspoon pepper, garlic powder and egg. Mix by hand until well combined. Form mixture into 12 balls, cover and store in refrigerator. In a large saucepan over medium heat, sauté onion and garlic in olive oil until onion is translucent. Stir in whole tomatoes in juice, salt, sugar and bay leaf. Cover, reduce heat to low and let simmer for 90 minutes. Stir in tomato paste, basil, remaining ½ teaspoon pepper and meatballs. Continue to simmer for 30 minutes or until meatballs are cooked through. Makes 6 servings.

Cheese & Beef Stuffed Shells

1 (12 oz.) pkg. uncooked jumbo
   pasta shells
3 lbs. ground beef
2 eggs, lightly beaten
2 T. olive oil
2 tsp. minced garlic

2 tsp. garlic salt
2 tsp. dried parsley
1 (8 oz.) pkg. cream cheese, softened
2 (14 oz.) jars pasta sauce, divided
½ C. grated Romano cheese

In a large pot of lightly salted water over medium heat, bring water to a boil. Add pasta shells and cook for 8 to 10 minutes or until pasta is al dente. Drain water from pot and set aside cooked shells. Preheat oven to 375° and lightly grease a 9 x 13″ baking dish. In a medium skillet over medium heat, combine ground beef, eggs, olive oil, minced garlic, garlic salt and parsley. Cook until beef is evenly browned. Drain grease from skillet and transfer beef mixture to a large bowl. Add cream cheese and 1 cup pasta sauce; mix well. Stuff the cooked pasta shells with the beef mixture and arrange, stuffed side up, in the baking dish. Pour desired amount of the remaining pasta sauce over shells. Bake for 15 minutes or until sauce is bubbly. Before serving, sprinkle with Romano cheese. Makes 8 servings.

Cheesy Chicken Linguine

2 T. olive oil

1 lb. skinless, boneless chicken breast halves, cut into strips

2 red bell peppers, sliced

2 C. milk

½ C. butter

1½ to 2 C. shredded Muenster cheese

1 clove garlic, minced

2 T. cornstarch

1 (16 oz.) pkg. uncooked linguine pasta

¼ tsp. garlic powder

In a large skillet over medium heat, place olive oil. Once oil is hot, add chicken strips and sauté until golden brown. Add sliced bell peppers and cook until they become limp. Cover saucepan and let simmer. Meanwhile, in a medium saucepan over high heat, combine milk, butter, shredded cheese and minced garlic. Heat for 10 minutes, stirring constantly to avoid burning. If sauce is not thick, add cornstarch in 1 teaspoon increments until desired consistency is achieved. In a large pot of lightly salted water over medium heat, bring water to a boil. Add linguine and cook for 8 to 10 minutes or until pasta is al dente. Drain water from pot. Add chicken and peppers to linguine in pot. Pour sauce over pasta and season with garlic powder. Toss all together and serve hot. Makes 4 servings.

Garlic Chicken Florentine with Pesto

2 T. olive oil
2 cloves garlic, minced
4 skinless, boneless chicken breast
    halves, cut into strips
2 C. chopped fresh spinach

1 (4.5 oz.) pkg. dry Alfredo sauce mix
2 T. pesto
1 (8 oz.) pkg. uncooked penne pasta
1 T. grated Romano cheese

In a large skillet over medium-high heat, place olive oil. Once oil is hot, add minced garlic and sauté for 1 minute. Add chicken strips and cook for 7 to 8 minutes on each side. When chicken is almost completely cooked through, add spinach and sauté for an additional 3 to 4 minutes. Meanwhile, prepare Alfredo sauce according to package directions. Stir pesto into the prepared Alfredo sauce and set aside. In a large pot of lightly salted water over medium heat, bring water to a boil. Add penne pasta and cook for 8 to 10 minutes or until pasta is al dente. Rinse pasta under cold water and drain. Add garlic, chicken and spinach to pasta. Pour pesto Alfredo sauce over pasta and toss together. Sprinkle Romano cheese on top. Makes 4 servings.

Mozzarella Garlic Chicken

3 T. olive oil
2 skinless, boneless chicken
    breast halves
1 T. garlic powder

1 clove garlic, minced
6 fresh mushrooms, sliced
2 C. shredded mozzarella cheese

In a medium skillet over medium heat, place olive oil. Season both sides of the chicken breast halves with garlic powder and minced garlic. Add chicken to skillet and cook for 12 minutes on each side or until juices run clear and chicken is cooked through. Set chicken aside and keep warm. In same skillet over medium heat, place sliced mushrooms and sauté until tender. Return chicken breast halves to skillet and layer mushrooms over top. Sprinkle mozzarella cheese over top and heat until cheese is melted, about 5 minutes. Makes 2 servings.

Lemon Garlic Chicken Skewers

½ C. low-fat lemon-flavored yogurt
⅓ C. rice wine vinegar
1 (1˝) piece fresh gingerroot, minced
2 cloves garlic, minced
1 tsp. ground cumin
¼ tsp. pumpkin pie spice

½ tsp. salt
¼ tsp. pepper
1½ lbs. skinless, boneless chicken
thighs or breasts
Wooden skewers

In a glass or stainless steel bowl, combine yogurt, rice wine vinegar, minced gingerroot, minced garlic, cumin, pumpkin pie spice, salt and pepper. Pound chicken to ½˝ thickness and cut chicken into 1½˝ wide strips. Add chicken to yogurt mixture and toss until well coated. Cover bowl and refrigerate at least 20 minutes or up to 24 hours. Preheat oven broiler or outdoor grill to medium-high heat. Soak the wooden skewers in hot water for 15 minutes. Thread coated chicken onto skewers; discard marinade. Grill or broil chicken skewers until no longer pink in the center, about 3 to 4 minutes. Makes 4 servings.

Cheesy Herbed Chicken

2 (15 oz.) cans tomato sauce
1 (6 oz.) can tomato paste
1 T. sugar
1 tsp. dried parsley
1 tsp. dried basil
1 tsp. dried oregano
1 medium clove garlic, minced

1 C. fine dry bread crumbs
3 lbs. skinless, boneless chicken
    breast halves
Garlic salt to taste
Salt and pepper to taste
1 lb. shredded Cheddar cheese, divided
1 lb. mozzarella cheese, divided

Preheat oven to 350°. Lightly grease two 9 x 13″ baking dishes. In a large pot over medium heat, combine tomato sauce, tomato paste, sugar, parsley, basil, oregano and minced garlic. Place bread crumbs in a large shallow dish. Place chicken in bread crumbs, turning to coat both sides. Transfer chicken breast halves to the baking dishes and sprinkle with garlic salt, salt and pepper to taste. Sprinkle half of the Cheddar cheese and half of the mozzarella cheese over the chicken. Pour tomato sauce evenly over chicken. Cover dishes with aluminum foil and bake for 50 minutes or until chicken is cooked through. Remove foil and sprinkle remaining cheeses over chicken. Return dish to oven and cook, uncovered, until cheese is melted. Makes 12 servings.

Breaded Cheddar Chicken

½ C. butter
4 cloves garlic, minced
¾ C. dry bread crumbs
½ C. grated Parmesan cheese
1½ C. shredded Cheddar cheese
¼ tsp. dried parsley

¼ tsp. dried oregano
⅛ tsp. salt
¼ tsp. pepper
8 skinless, boneless chicken
   breast halves

Preheat oven to 350°. In a medium saucepan over low heat, place butter. Once butter is melted, add minced garlic and sauté until tender, about 5 minutes. Place bread crumbs in a large shallow dish and add Parmesan cheese, Cheddar cheese, parsley, oregano, salt and pepper; mix until well combined. Pound chicken to 1½″ thickness. Dip chicken breast halves into the garlic butter and then into bread crumb mixture, turning to coat both sides. Arrange coated chicken in a 9 x 13″ baking dish. Bake for 30 minutes or until juices run clear and chicken is cooked through. Makes 8 servings.

Baked Rosemary Chicken

1 lemon
1 C. butter, softened
3 T. minced garlic
¼ C. chopped fresh rosemary
1 (3 lb.) whole chicken

Salt and pepper to taste
1 tsp. paprika
5 sprigs fresh rosemary
5 cloves garlic, minced

Preheat oven to 350°. Rinse the chicken and pat dry. Zest the lemon and slice the remaining lemon into quarters. In a medium bowl, combine butter, lemon zest, 3 tablespoons minced garlic and the ¼ cup chopped rosemary. Spread the butter mixture between the skin and meat of the whole chicken by loosening the skin and creating "pockets" around the breast, legs and wings. Season the cavity of the chicken with salt, pepper and paprika. Add the quartered lemon, rosemary sprigs and garlic cloves to the chicken cavity. Bind the legs and tuck the wings into the leg joints. Place the chicken on a roasting rack, breast side up. Roast for approximately 50 minutes or until the juices run clear. Remove and discard lemon, rosemary sprigs and garlic cloves. Makes 5 to 6 servings.

Marinated Garlic Chicken

1 egg yolk
6 cloves garlic, minced
4 skinless, boneless chicken breast
    halves
6 T. butter, melted
1 C. dry bread crumbs

1 C. grated Parmesan cheese
1 T. dried parsley
1 T. garlic powder
½ T. salt
1 T. pepper

In a glass bowl, beat egg yolk with minced garlic. Add chicken breast halves to bowl and toss to coat. Cover dish and refrigerate at least 4 hours or up to 24 hours. Preheat oven to 400°. In a 9 x 13″ baking dish combine melted butter, bread crumbs, Parmesan cheese, parsley, garlic powder, salt and pepper. Dip marinated chicken in crumb mixture, turning to coat both sides. Pour remaining garlic mixture over top. Bake for 20 minutes. Turn chicken breast halves over and return to oven for an additional 20 minutes or until chicken is cooked through. Makes 4 servings.

Chicken Stuffed Braid

2 C. cooked, diced chicken
1 C. chopped broccoli
½ C. chopped red bell pepper
1 clove garlic, crushed
1 C. shredded Cheddar cheese
½ C. mayonnaise

2 tsp. dried dillweed
¼ tsp. salt
2 T. slivered almonds
¼ C. diced onion
2 (8 oz.) tubes refrigerated crescent rolls
1 egg white, beaten

Preheat oven to 375°. In a large bowl, combine diced chicken, broccoli, red bell pepper, garlic, Cheddar cheese, mayonnaise, dillweed, salt, almonds and onion; mix well. Unroll crescent roll dough and arrange on a baking sheet. Pinch together perforations to form a single sheet of dough. Using kitchen shears or a pizza wheel, cut 1″ wide strips on both sides of the dough toward the center, making sure to leave a solid 3″ wide strip of dough down the center. Spread chicken mixture evenly over the center strip. Fold the side strips over the chicken mixture, alternating to look like a braid. Pinch or twist the strips to seal. Brush with egg white. Bake for 25 to 28 minutes or until dough is golden brown. Makes 6 servings.

Grilled Ginger Pork Chops

½ C. orange juice
2 T. soy sauce
2 T. minced fresh gingerroot
2 T. orange zest

1 tsp. minced garlic
1 tsp. garlic-flavored chile paste
½ tsp. salt
6 (½″ thick) pork loin chops

In a 9 x 13″ baking dish, combine orange juice, soy sauce, minced gingerroot, orange zest, minced garlic, chile paste and salt; mix until well combined. Add pork chops to baking dish, turning to coat evenly. Cover dish and refrigerate at least 2 hours or up to 12 hours, turning the chops occasionally. Preheat grill to high heat and lightly oil the grate. Grill pork chops for 5 to 6 minutes on each side or to desired doneness.

Slow-Cooked Pork Chops

¼ C. olive oil

1 C. chicken broth

2 cloves garlic, minced

1 T. paprika

1 T. garlic powder

1 T. poultry seasoning

1 tsp. dried oregano

1 tsp. dried basil

4 thick-cut boneless pork chops

Salt and pepper to taste

In a large bowl, whisk together olive oil, chicken broth, minced garlic, paprika, garlic powder, poultry seasoning, oregano and basil; mix well and pour into a slow cooker. Using a sharp knife, cut slits in each pork chop and season both sides with salt and pepper to taste. Place pork chops in the slow cooker. Cover with slow cooker lid and cook on high for 4 hours, basting occasionally with the sauce. Makes 4 servings.

Roasted Seasoned Pork Loin

1 tsp. dried sage	½ C. sugar
½ tsp. salt	1 T. cornstarch
¼ tsp. pepper	¼ C. white vinegar
1 clove garlic, crushed	¼ C. water
1 (5 lb.) boneless pork loin	2 T. soy sauce

Preheat oven to 325°. In a small bowl, combine sage, salt, pepper and crushed garlic. Mix well and rub seasonings all over the pork loin. Place pork in an uncovered roasting pan on the middle oven rack. Bake for 3 hours or until the internal temperature of the pork reaches at least 150° on a meat thermometer. Meanwhile, in a small saucepan over medium heat, combine sugar, cornstarch, vinegar, water and soy sauce. Heat, stirring occasionally, until mixture begins to simmer and thicken slightly. Brush glaze mixture over pork 3 or 4 times during last 30 minutes of baking time. Before serving, pour any remaining glaze over pork. Makes 8 servings.

Smoked Baby Back Ribs

5 lbs. baby back pork ribs
½ gallon apple juice
1 head garlic, separated into cloves

2 C. barbecue sauce
1 T. garlic salt

Prepare an outdoor smoker by filling with charcoal and heating to 225°. Cut ribs into portions of 3 or 4 ribs each. Place rib sections in a large pot and fill with enough apple juice to just cover the ribs. Place the lid on the pot and bring to a boil over medium-high heat. Remove from heat and let stand for 15 minutes. Lightly oil the grate of the smoker and place ribs on the grate. Toss a few garlic cloves into the hot coals and close the smoker. Maintain the temperature at 225° by adding more charcoal as needed. Smoke the ribs for 7 hours, adding more garlic cloves to the coals occasionally. To make the sauce, combine barbecue sauce with a little apple juice and season with garlic salt. Baste ribs with sauce and continue cooking for 30 minutes. Makes 5 to 6 servings.

Garlic Prime Rib

1 (10 lb.) prime rib roast
6 cloves garlic, sliced

Salt and pepper to taste
½ C. Dijon mustard

Preheat oven to 500°. Using a sharp knife, cut small slits in the roast. Insert 1 garlic slice into each slit. Season the roast with salt and pepper to taste and spread Dijon mustard over all. Place roast on a rack in a roasting pan and cover. Roast for 60 minutes. Turn off oven and leave the door closed. Allow roast to sit in oven for an additional 90 minutes. The internal temperature of the roast should be at least 140° for medium-rare and 155° for medium. Makes 12 servings.

Sirloin with Garlic Butter

½ C. butter
2 tsp. garlic powder
4 cloves garlic, minced

8 top sirloin beef steaks
Salt and pepper to taste

Preheat an outdoor grill to high heat. In a small saucepan over medium-low heat, place butter. Once butter is melted, stir in garlic powder and minced garlic. Sauté for 1 to 2 minutes and set aside. Sprinkle both sides of each steak with salt and pepper. Grill steaks for 4 to 5 minutes per side or to desired doneness. Transfer cooked steaks to a warmed, clean plate. Brush a generous amount of the butter and garlic mixture over each steak. Makes 8 servings.

Beef Brisket with 40 Garlic Cloves

1 (5 to 6 lb.) beef brisket
Coarse salt and pepper to taste
2 T. olive oil
40 large cloves garlic, peeled
1 large sweet onion, sliced and
   separated into rings

¼ C. red wine vinegar
2 to 3 C. beef broth
2 tsp. dried oregano
1 tsp. dried basil

Preheat oven to 325°. Rinse the beef brisket and pat dry. Season brisket generously with coarse salt and pepper. In a large Dutch oven or oven-proof skillet, place olive oil, turning to coat the bottom; place over medium-high heat. Once the pan is hot, sear all sides of the brisket until golden brown and remove to a platter. Add garlic cloves and onion rings to the remaining oil in the pan, sautéing until garlic begins to turn golden and onions are limp. Add vinegar to deglaze the pan, stirring for 1 minute. Add beef broth, oregano and basil. Bring to a simmer and turn off heat. Move onions and garlic

continued on next page

to the side and return brisket to the pan. Spoon garlic and onions over the brisket, cover pan tightly and place in oven. Bake for 1 hour. Reduce oven temperature to 300° and bake for an additional 1½ to 2 hours or until brisket is tender. Remove brisket to a platter and keep warm. Remove onions and half of the garlic cloves to a bowl. Skim excess oil from the pan gravy and discard. Blend pan gravy and remaining garlic until smooth, adding flour or cornstarch to thicken the gravy if desired. Return onions and garlic to the gravy. Slice brisket diagonally and serve with gravy. Makes 8 to 10 servings.

Sweet Glazed Salmon

2 T. olive oil
1 tsp. water
½ C. red wine vinegar
2 cloves garlic, crushed
1 tsp. garlic salt

½ tsp. pepper
2 tsp. dried basil
1 (1⅓ lb.) salmon fillet
½ C. sugar

In a 9 x 13″ baking dish, combine olive oil, water, red wine vinegar, crushed garlic, garlic salt, pepper and basil. Place salmon fillet in marinade, meat side down. Cover and refrigerate for 30 minutes. Preheat an outdoor grill to medium heat and lightly oil the grate. Coat salmon fillet lightly with sugar. Place fillet on grill, skin side down, and cook for 18 to 20 minutes. Do not turn salmon over. Baste with remaining marinade occasionally during cooking. Salmon is done when it flakes easily with a fork. Makes 4 servings.

Garlic Lime Salmon

3 cloves garlic
3 T. fresh grated gingerroot
2 jalapeno peppers, seeded and sliced
½ C. fresh chopped cilantro

3 T. lime juice
1 T. olive oil
½ tsp. salt
4 (¼ to ½ lb.) salmon fillets

In a blender or food processor, combine garlic cloves, gingerroot, jalapeno slices, cilantro, lime juice, olive oil and salt. Pulse until smooth and well blended. Coat each salmon fillet with a generous amount of the blended mixture and marinate in refrigerator for 30 minutes. Heat a large skillet over medium heat. Add coated salmon fillets to hot skillet, cover and cook for 5 to 10 minutes or until salmon flakes easily with a fork. Be careful not to overcook the salmon or it will dry out. Makes 4 servings.

Salmon Patties

1 (14.75 oz.) can salmon, drained
   and flaked
2 eggs, beaten
¼ C. garlic-flavored dry bread crumbs
¼ C. dry potato flakes
1 medium onion, finely diced

1 clove garlic, minced
¼ tsp. dried dillweed
¼ tsp. celery salt
Salt and pepper to taste
2 T. olive oil

In a medium bowl, combine flaked salmon, eggs, bread crumbs, potato flakes, diced onion, minced garlic, dillweed, celery salt, salt and pepper. Mix until well combined and form mixture into 2″ balls. Flatten each ball into a ½″ thick patty. In a medium skillet over medium heat, heat olive oil. Add patties to the skillet, a few at a time, and cook until lightly browned, about 5 minutes on each side.

Baked Garlic Trout

1 (10 oz.) trout
1 clove garlic, minced
¼ yellow onion, chopped
½ lemon, juiced

1 tsp. butter
½ tsp. garlic salt
Salt and pepper to taste
½ jalapeno pepper, seeded and diced

Preheat oven to 400°. Clean the trout, removing the head and tail. Fill the cavity of the trout with the minced garlic, chopped onion and lemon juice. Rub butter over the outside of the trout and place on a large piece of foil. Season trout with garlic salt, salt and pepper to taste. Place diced jalapeno peppers over trout and seal the trout in the foil. Place foil-wrapped trout directly on an oven rack and bake for 25 minutes or until the fish flakes easily with a fork. Makes 1 to 2 servings.

Grilled Sea Bass

¼ tsp. garlic powder
¼ tsp. onion powder
¼ tsp. paprika
Lemon pepper to taste
Coarse salt to taste

2 lbs. sea bass
3 T. butter
2 large cloves garlic, minced
1 T. chopped fresh parsley
1½ T. extra-virgin olive oil

Preheat an outdoor grill to high heat and lightly oil the grate. In a small bowl, combine garlic powder, onion powder, paprika, lemon pepper and salt. Mix well and sprinkle seasonings over fish. In a small saucepan over medium heat, place butter, minced garlic and parsley. Once the butter has melted, remove saucepan from heat. Grill fish for 7 minutes. Turn fish over and drizzle with butter mixture. Continue to grill for an additional 7 minutes or until fish flakes easily with a fork. Drizzle with olive oil just before serving. Makes 6 servings.

Garlic Shrimp

⅓ C. butter
1½ to 2 lbs. large shrimp, peeled
    and deveined
4 to 6 medium cloves garlic, minced

⅓ C. chopped fresh parsley
2½ T. lemon juice
Salt to taste

In a large skillet over medium heat, place butter. Heat until butter is melted and stops foaming, about 30 to 45 seconds. Add shrimp and garlic and sauté until shrimp just turn pink, about 4 to 5 minutes. Add the parsley, lemon juice and salt and mix well. Serve immediately. Makes 4 to 6 servings.

Marinated Grilled Shrimp Skewers

3 cloves garlic, minced
⅓ C. olive oil
¼ C. tomato sauce
2 T. red wine vinegar
2 T. chopped fresh basil

½ tsp. salt
¼ tsp. cayenne pepper
2 lbs. shrimp, peeled and deveined
Wooden skewers

In a large bowl, combine minced garlic, olive oil, tomato sauce and red wine vinegar. Mix in basil, salt and cayenne pepper. Add shrimp to bowl, tossing until evenly coated. Cover and refrigerate for 30 minutes to 1 hour, stirring occasionally. Soak the wooden skewers in hot water for 15 minutes. Preheat an outdoor grill to medium heat and lightly oil the grate. Thread marinated shrimp onto the skewers, piercing each shrimp once near the tail and once near the head. Discard remaining marinade. Cook shrimp skewers for 2 to 3 minutes per side or until shrimp turn pink. Makes 6 servings.

Cornbread Fried Shrimp

1 (7.5 oz.) box cornbread muffin mix
1 tsp. onion powder
1 tsp. garlic powder
½ tsp. lemon pepper
½ tsp. chili powder or cayenne pepper
½ tsp. paprika

½ tsp. ground cumin
1 tsp. salt
1 C. buttermilk
1 lb. shrimp, peeled and deveined
Peanut oil

In a medium bowl, combine cornbread muffin mix, onion powder, garlic powder, lemon pepper, chili powder, paprika, cumin and salt; mix well. Pour buttermilk into a small bowl. Dip the shrimp into the buttermilk and then into the cornbread mixture, shaking off any excess. Place coated shrimp on a baking sheet and chill in refrigerator for 1 hour. In a deep-fryer or deep skillet, preheat peanut oil to 375°. Add coated shrimp to hot oil, a few at a time, until coating is golden brown. Remove shrimp to paper towels to drain. Serve immediately. Makes 4 servings.

Baked Scallops

4 T. butter, melted
1½ lbs. bay scallops, rinsed and drained
½ C. dry bread crumbs
1 tsp. onion powder
1 tsp. garlic powder

½ tsp. paprika
½ tsp. dried parsley
3 cloves garlic, minced
¼ C. grated Parmesan cheese

Preheat oven to 400°. In a 2-quart casserole dish, place melted butter. Add scallops and toss until coated in butter; spread evenly. In a medium bowl, combine bread crumbs, onion powder, garlic powder, paprika, parsley, minced garlic and Parmesan cheese; mix well. Sprinkle mixture over scallops. Bake for 20 minutes or until scallops are firm. Makes 4 servings.

Soups

Tomato Soup with Zucchini

2½ T. olive oil
1 medium zucchini, cubed
1 clove garlic, minced
8 large tomatoes, cored
1 small sweet onion, chopped
1 small red chile pepper, chopped

1 (14 oz.) can vegetable broth
1 T. dried tarragon
2 tsp. dried dillweed
1 tsp. salt
¼ tsp. pepper

In a medium skillet over medium heat, place olive oil. Add cubed zucchini and minced garlic and cook until lightly browned. Remove from heat and set aside. In a blender or food processor, place the tomatoes, onion and chile pepper. Blend until well combined, leaving a few small chunks, if desired. In a large pot over medium heat, combine tomato puree and vegetable broth. Mix in tarragon, dillweed, salt and pepper. Bring to a boil, reduce heat to low and mix in zucchini and garlic. Cover and simmer for 45 minutes. Makes 8 servings.

Garbanzo Bean Stew

1½ C. dry garbanzo beans
10 C. vegetable broth
½ tsp. crushed red pepper flakes
4 cloves garlic, minced, divided
1 tsp. vegetable oil
2 lbs. tomatoes, chopped

1 C. chopped fresh basil
2 lbs. fresh fennel bulbs, trimmed
  and chopped
2 medium onions, chopped
½ tsp. salt
1 C. fresh green peas

In a large pot, place garbanzo beans. Add enough water to cover beans and let soak at least 8 hours or overnight. Drain beans and rinse under water. In a large pot over medium-high heat, combine drained beans, vegetable broth, red pepper flakes and half of the minced garlic. Bring to a boil, reduce heat to low and let simmer for 45 minutes or until beans are tender. In a large skillet over medium heat, place oil. Once oil is hot, add remaining minced garlic, tomatoes and basil. Heat for 2 minutes or until the basil is just wilted. Remove from heat and set aside. Add the fennel and onions to the garbanzo bean mixture. Season with salt and cook for 15 more minutes. Mix in the tomato mixture and peas and heat for 5 minutes or until peas are tender. Makes 6 servings.

Garlic Soup with Cilantro Dumplings

2 heads garlic, peeled and minced
8 C. water
3 stalks celery, finely chopped
3 carrots, cut into 1″ pieces
1 T. dried parsley
1 tsp. dried basil
1 bay leaf
Salt and pepper to taste

1⅓ C. flour
½ tsp. salt
2 tsp. baking powder
2 T. chopped fresh cilantro
¼ tsp. pepper
1 egg, beaten
1½ T. vegetable oil
⅓ C. milk

In a large pot over medium heat, combine minced garlic, water, celery, carrots, parsley, basil, bay leaf, salt and pepper. Bring to a simmer for 30 minutes. Meanwhile, in a medium bowl, combine flour, salt, baking powder, cilantro and pepper. Mix well and add egg, vegetable oil and milk. Drop very small teaspoonfuls of the dough into the simmering soup. When the dumplings float to the top, after 1 or 2 minutes, the soup is ready to be served. Makes 6 to 8 servings.

Roasted Garlic Soup

4 heads garlic
Olive oil
Salt and pepper to taste
3 C. milk

1 C. heavy cream
Chopped fresh thyme to taste
Croutons

Preheat oven to 350°. Place heads of garlic on a baking sheet. Drizzle with olive oil and sprinkle with salt and pepper. Roast in oven for 45 minutes or until cloves are golden brown. Cut the roasted garlic heads in half sideways. Squeeze the cloves out of each half into a large saucepan, removing any peelings or fibers. Add the milk, heavy cream and thyme to the saucepan and place over medium heat. Bring to a simmer for 10 minutes. Transfer mixture to a blender or food processor and puree until smooth. Strain liquid back into saucepan through a fine-holed sieve. Season with additional salt and pepper to taste. Ladle soup into bowls. Float a few croutons in each bowl and drizzle lightly with olive oil. Makes 4 servings.

Southwestern Garlic Soup

3 heads garlic
3 T. peanut oil, divided
1 medium onion, thinly sliced
8 C. vegetable broth
1 to 2 dried chipotle chilies

½ tsp. salt
½ tsp. cumin seeds
Juice of 1 lime
Small tortilla chips and avocado slices,
   for garnish

Preheat oven to 400°. Place heads of garlic on a baking sheet. Rub garlic heads with 1 tablespoon peanut oil and roast in oven for 45 minutes or until cloves are golden brown. Remove from oven and let garlic cool. Peel all the cloves. In a large saucepan over medium heat, place 1 tablespoon peanut oil. Add onion and sauté until softened. Transfer sautéed onions and garlic cloves to a blender or food processor and puree until smooth. Add remaining 1 tablespoon peanut oil to saucepan over medium-high heat. Pour in the blended mixture and heat just until puree begins to darken in color. Add vegetable broth, chilies, salt and cumin seeds. Reduce heat to medium and simmer for 25 to 30 minutes. Remove from heat and stir in lime juice. Ladle soup into bowls and garnish each serving with a few tortilla chips and avocado slices. Makes 6 to 8 servings.

Carrot Potato Soup

1 T. vegetable oil
1 large onion, diced
3 cloves garlic, minced
4 large carrots, sliced
5 new potatoes, quartered

2 C. vegetable broth
2 tsp. grated fresh gingerroot
1 tsp. curry powder
Salt and pepper to taste

In a medium pot over medium heat, place vegetable oil. Add onion and garlic; sauté until tender. Add sliced carrots and quartered potatoes and heat until carrots begin to sweat. Add vegetable broth, gingerroot, curry powder, salt and pepper. Bring to a boil, reduce heat to low and let simmer for 15 to 20 minutes or until carrots are tender. In a blender or food processor, puree soup in batches until smooth. Return pureed soup to pot over low heat and ladle soup into bowls. Makes 4 servings.

Roasted Confetti Soup

1 green bell pepper
1 large red bell pepper
1 large orange bell pepper
1 yellow bell pepper
8 cloves garlic
Juice of 1 small lemon

3 C. vegetable broth
1 tsp. fennel seed
¼ tsp. dried thyme
¼ tsp. garlic salt
Pepper to taste

Preheat oven to 375°. Cut all of the peppers in half and remove the seeds. Peel the garlic cloves. Place peppers, cut side up, in a shallow baking dish. Place 1 garlic clove in each pepper half and sprinkle lemon juice over peppers. Roast in oven for 1 hour. Remove peppers from oven and let cool. Once cooled, peel the skin from the peppers. Meanwhile, in a large saucepan over medium heat, place vegetable broth and fennel seeds. Bring to a boil, reduce heat, cover and let simmer until peppers are done baking. Strain the fennel seeds from the broth and return to a boil. Add thyme and simmer for 15 minutes. Slice a 1″ section from each pepper, chop and set aside for garnish. In a blender or food processor, place remaining peppers with garlic cloves and ½ cup hot broth; pulse a few times but do not puree. Add blended mixture to broth; stir well and season with garlic salt and pepper. Ladle soup into bowls and garnish with reserved chopped peppers.

Creamed Corn Soup

½ onion, chopped
1 clove garlic, minced
¼ C. chopped fresh parsley
1 T. butter
3 T. flour
2½ C. milk
1 C. chicken broth

2 (12 oz.) cans whole kernel corn, drained
2½ T. cream cheese
1 tsp. garlic salt
1 tsp. pepper
Cayenne pepper to taste

In a large pot over medium heat, combine onion, garlic, parsley and butter. Sauté for 5 minutes or until onions are tender. Stir in flour, mixing well. Whisk in milk and chicken broth. Add the corn and cream cheese and heat until cream cheese is completely melted. Season with garlic salt, pepper and cayenne pepper. Mix well and serve hot. Makes 4 servings.

Vegetable Bacon Fagioli

1 (29 oz.) can diced tomatoes, drained
2 (14 oz.) cans Great Northern
    beans in liquid
1 (14 oz.) can chopped spinach, drained
2 (14.5 oz.) cans chicken broth
1 (8 oz.) can tomato sauce
3 C. water
1 T. minced garlic

8 slices bacon, cooked and crumbled
1 T. dried parsley
1 tsp. garlic powder
1½ tsp. salt
½ tsp. pepper
½ tsp. dried basil
8 oz. uncooked shell pasta
Grated Romano cheese

In a large pot over medium heat, combine diced tomatoes, Northern beans and liquid, spinach, chicken broth, tomato sauce, water, minced garlic, crumbled bacon, parsley, garlic powder, salt, pepper and basil. Bring to a boil, reduce heat, cover and let simmer for 40 minutes. Add shell pasta and heat until pasta is tender, about 10 minutes. Ladle soup into bowls and garnish with Romano cheese. Makes 8 servings.

Poached Garlic Soup

30 cloves garlic, peeled
7 C. vegetable or chicken broth, divided
½ C. plus 6 T. butter, divided
½ C. chopped onion
8 small new potatoes, peeled and diced

Salt and pepper to taste
1 C. heavy cream
1 C. milk
6 small slices sourdough bread
Grated Parmesan cheese

In a medium saucepan over medium-high heat, combine garlic cloves and 3 cups broth. Bring to a boil for 15 minutes or until garlic cloves are soft. Remove garlic cloves to a small bowl and add 6 tablespoons butter; mash into a paste and set aside. Reduce broth in saucepan to a glaze and set aside. In a large pot over low heat, melt remaining ½ cup butter. Add onion and potatoes and sauté until soft. Season with salt and pepper and add remaining 4 cups broth. Increase heat to medium-high and simmer for 25 minutes or until potatoes are softened. Transfer mixture to a blender and puree until smooth; return to pot over low heat. Add glaze and stir until well blended. Mix in heavy cream and milk; season with salt and pepper to taste. Preheat broiler. Spread garlic paste over bread slices and toast under a broiler for 1 minute. Ladle soup into 6 bowls. Float 1 toasted garlic bread in each bowl and sprinkle with Parmesan cheese. Makes 6 servings.

Creamy Potato & Rosemary Soup

2 T. olive oil

1½ lbs. russet potatoes, peeled and cut into 1″ cubes

1 large onion, diced

1 T. butter

Pinch of sugar

3 cloves garlic, sliced

⅛ tsp. cayenne pepper

3 C. chicken broth

1½ tsp. minced fresh rosemary

1½ C. half-and-half, divided

Salt and pepper to taste

In a large, deep saucepan over medium-high heat, place olive oil. Add potatoes and onions and sauté for 7 to 8 minutes or until potatoes start to turn light brown. Reduce heat to low and add butter, sugar and garlic. Continue to sauté for 10 minutes or until vegetables turn a caramel color. Add cayenne pepper and sauté for 30 seconds. Stir in broth and bring to a simmer. Reduce heat to low and continue to simmer until potatoes are tender, about 10 minutes. Transfer mixture to a blender and add rosemary. Puree until well blended and smooth. Add a little half-and-half and blend for a few more seconds. Return to saucepan or medium pot over medium heat. Add remaining half-and-half and season with salt and pepper to taste. Ladle into bowls and serve hot. Makes 8 servings.

Slow-Cooked Veggie Beef Stew

1 lb. ground beef
2 cloves garlic, minced
1 small onion, diced
1 green bell pepper, diced
3 stalks celery, diced
1 (28 oz.) can Italian-style stewed
    tomatoes, drained
1 (15 oz.) can mixed vegetables,
    drained

8 C. beef broth
3 T. soy sauce
2 T. Worcestershire sauce
¾ tsp. paprika
Salt and pepper to taste
6 oz. uncooked spiral pasta

In a large skillet over medium heat, cook ground beef until lightly browned. Mix in garlic, onion and green bell pepper. Cook, stirring often, until beef is evenly browned and vegetables are tender. Drain grease from saucepan and transfer beef and vegetables to a slow cooker. Add celery, drained tomatoes and drained mixed vegetables to slow cooker. Pour in beef broth, soy sauce and Worcestershire sauce. Season with paprika, salt and pepper. Cover slow cooker with lid and cook on high for 7 hours. Stir in uncooked pasta during last 15 minutes of cooking time. Makes 8 servings.

Seasoned Shrimp Soup

8 C. chicken broth
2 T. dried rosemary
5 cloves garlic, minced
1 tsp. pepper
1 tsp. celery seed
½ tsp. fennel seed

1 C. clam juice
½ (6 oz.) can tomato paste
1 C. butter
1 C. white wine
2 lbs. shrimp, peeled and deveined
1 (1 lb.) loaf French bread

In a large pot, combine chicken broth, rosemary, garlic, pepper, celery seed, fennel seed, clam juice, tomato paste and butter. Bring to a boil, reduce heat to low and let simmer for 1 hour, stirring occasionally. Mix white wine into soup and continue to simmer for 2 hours. Just before serving, stir in shrimp and cook for 3 minutes or until shrimp turn opaque. Ladle soup into bowls and serve with French bread for soaking up the broth. Makes 8 servings.

Dessert

Garlic Ice Cream

3 C. whole milk
¼ tsp. crushed garlic
1 vanilla bean, split

1 C. heavy cream
1½ C. sugar
9 egg yolks

In a medium saucepan over medium-low heat, combine milk, crushed garlic and vanilla bean. Bring to a slow boil and remove from heat. Pour liquid into a medium bowl through a strainer, removing any garlic peels and vanilla bean pods. In a large bowl, combine heavy cream, sugar and egg yolks. Mix well. Pour strained milk mixture into the cream mixture, stirring constantly. Transfer mixture to a medium saucepan over medium heat. Cook, stirring often, until mixture has thickened and coats the back of a spoon, about 10 to 15 minutes. Fill a large bowl with ice water. Remove saucepan from heat and dip the bottom of the saucepan into the ice water to cool the mixture. Transfer cream to an ice cream freezer and follow manufacturer's directions for freezing the ice cream. Makes 8 servings.

Index

Appetizers & Sauces

Breads

Side Dishes

Main Dishes

Artichoke Pie 53
Bacon, Pea & Garlic Spaghetti 58
Baked Garlic Trout 85
Baked Rosemary Chicken 71
Baked Scallops 90
Beef Brisket with 40 Garlic Cloves 80
Breaded Cheddar Chicken 70
Cheese & Beef Stuffed Shells 64
Cheesy Chicken Linguine 65
Cheesy Herbed Chicken 69
Chicken Stuffed Braid 73
Cornbread Fried Shrimp 89
Deep-Dish Broccoli Pizza 54
Easy Chicken Pasta Toss 61
Egg & Sausage Muffins 51
Garlic Chicken Florentine with Pesto...66
Garlic Lime Salmon 83
Garlic Penne Pasta...57
Garlic Prime Rib 78

Soups

Dessert